SEEKING GRACE

Faye Snider

LILY POETRY REVIEW BOOKS

Dedicated to family,
past, present
and future

Table of Contents

Voice

Mornings, Maya comes to our bed,
cuddles between us, chats, plans.

She jumps every time the phone rings.
If it's one of them, I say, *Don't call back.*

In time, she does the same.

Proud as a vocalist singing her first solo,
she is taking hold, her voice strong
as a clarion bell.

Prologue

Thieves of the spirit,
their snake-like tongues
twist words of love
to capture
a lonely girl longing
for God's grace.

Maya, I am your mother.

I thought so long as God
was involved,
I didn't have to worry
about it being a cult,
you told me after.

Now, I understand.
You needed to believe
in yourself.

Lure

Barely twenty, in college,
Maya joins new friends
in the sanctuary room
where *mothers* and *fathers,*
uncles and *aunts* smile,
stroke her arms.

The local pastor's words:
Welcome to the pages
of the holy book
as taught by Dorian, our leader.

Your Jewish blood
will bring us
completion with Christ.

Manifesto

While Dorian sings
Marze-Eat Dotes and Doze Eat Oats
and Little Lambs Eat Ivy,
all around Maya— hands
furiously transcribe
his every word.

She will have to listen harder.

In the days that follow
her pen jots, scribbles,
fills her brain's pages
until she recites
every chapter, every verse
just as he does.

Dorian—
salesman-turned-preacher,
chosen by Jesus, baptized
in liquid waves of love
and anointed,
speaks for The Lord.

Dorian's Rules

Beware, the godless.
They are Disciples
of the Devil.

Beware. Our sister Martha,
turned to the sin of laxity.
Suffered a car accident.

Beware. Our brother Oliver,
abandoned prayer with us.
Wasting with cancer.

Beware. You who lust
in your automobiles
will never enter
The Kingdom of Heaven.

I am your true preacher.

Unbeknownst

to her father and me, she traverses the worlds
of her Jewish heritage and Dorian's teachings

in the mission to gather the vulnerable,
those loners she hands tracts on street corners,

those innocent mothers who open their doors
to the pretty young woman inviting them

to give over their children to the Bible preacher,
the ministry bus in wait at the curb,

a willing exchange for a half day of childcare.

Beware

In the cocoon of Dorian's kingdom
　　she rises before light.
　　　　Wrapped in group prayers,

and trilling like a skylark,
　　she chants his lyrics,
　　　　her mind set to *Beware*.

She comes to believe our laxity
　　lies in not knowing of Isaiah
　　　　and the messianic promise

that *trust in YHWH brings*
　　deliverance while those who
　　　　stray suffer judgment and pain.

Out of the Blue Maya Visits

I lost God in high school. As a little girl,
I prayed every night.

Now that I've found him, I'm very happy.
I don't understand why I never learned about Isaiah.
It's a mistake not to read the New Testament.

What is she saying?

I did not come to what I am about to tell you
without a lot of thought and study. I've learned about
Jesus. I believe in Jesus. I believe he is the Messiah
the Jews have been waiting for.

What is she saying?

Mom, I know this is hard on you.
That's why I waited and studied so hard.
Read. You will see.

You are a Jew. How can you
believe in Jesus?

I am a Jew and a Christian.
A completed Jew.

The First Time Maya Lost Her Voice

Overuse, too many rehearsals.
After performing in *West Side Story*,
voice raspy.

Why can't I sing high notes anymore?

Dear Maya,

I write this in preparation
for Rosh Hashanah.

I'm sorry for the pain I caused you—
the absent days, the moments
of loneliness, the fear and upset
with no arms to calm you.

I'm sorry for the tenderness lost in time.

Precious daughter,
will you forgive my absence?

As your mother, I should have known.

Her Father Decides a Visit

enters a makeshift sanctuary
reminiscent of the storefront
where he recited
his Bar Mitzvah speech
in Hebrew to people
much the same.

Maya,
next to the pastor,
renders a hymn
in her bravura voice
to Christ in Hebrew.

The pastor tells him,
If you read, if you pray with us,
you will feel the same way.

Where Is Our Curious Child

Why did Patty's daddy die?
It was his heart.

What's a bad heart?
When someone is very sick.

How does God make a rainbow?
He plays with light.

Where do frogs go in winter?
They sleep in the pond muck.

Have You Ever Found Yourself

in a maze, each corner turned,
each sunlit path, leading
to another turn

like that day in San Diego, far
from our tangled daughter.
We've come to explore

a job offer, perhaps for both of us.
I, smarting from her silence
to my "Dear Maya" letters,

her father, tired of seeking experts,
ready to leave the hurt of
Maya's enchantment behind.

On the beach, the sand hot on my feet,
my gut curls with shock—
my husband serious

about this leap,
a leap as shocking as Maya's.

I will have no part of his turning:
to embrace the west coast, he must
leave the east coast and me behind.

Two days later, we are homeward bound.

A Place In-between

When grandma asks,
What do you hear from her?
I blame myself.

Raised an Orthodox Jew,
I've become modern
and liberal, embrace
prayer books with English,
mix meat and milk.

When I can no longer
bear the silence
of Maya's voice—
its sound, a brook
tumbling into my own
sense of harmony,

I phone—
coffee in hand just before
dressing for work and later,
after dinner dishes until

she answers, her voice
trapped in surprise.

Cautiously, I invite her.
Cautiously, she agrees to meet,
I cannot quite believe.

The Reunion

The shape of her body
bloated in flesh of sallow patina,
her hair, once honey-colored
hangs dank, shrouds
her glossy eyes.

We greet as two strangers,
our conversation the weather
until she leans in,
speaks of a man,

older, divorced, her *friend*
in the *no touch-love* tradition
of Dorian's mission.
They met, *by God's will*
on the ministry bus.

She tells of a recent duck hunt,
my gentle child wearing
a bright orange vest,
eager to gather
bloodied creatures.

What of grandma, your brother,
aunts, uncles, and cousins?
They ask for you. They miss you.

I haven't seen them in two years.
They don't know me.
We're not really family.

Grandma?
She asks for you all the time.

I'll call her.

I offer gifts, a pair of earrings,
a soft sweatshirt, a journal,
in Chanukah wrap.
Who are they from?

Is that hope or relief
when she takes in my words,

                                From your father and me.

Afterwards

Alone on the highway,
I sense the grasp
of Dorian's tentacles as if
he's choked both of us.

Days later, a letter:

I know how scared you are
about driving on the highway
and I think it is fantastic
that you drove all the way to meet me.

Journal Entry: No Call Thus Far

Will she call Grandma? Or
will she shut out the light between the generations?

Calling Her Back

Dr. Clark says
Maya's personality,
folded tight
as a blossom in frost,
could be a sign
of her inability to choose,
even to leave.

If this is a destructive cult,
she could be thirty
before she awakens.
Maintain the connection
no matter what.

Asking Friends to Write, to Remind Her

Giancarlo, Maya's college roommate,
Remember the pizza parlor, how
we worked the last shift, savored
the sausage and pineapple tidbits?

Susan, Maya's childhood friend,
I miss our long talks.
Where are you?
Why can't I reach you?

Debbie, the college PT,
The weather here is brisk, perfect
for the intense walks you enjoy.
I hope you're taking care.

Prophecy

On the phone, Maya's voice,
matter of fact, announcing
her engagement to *the friend.*

Her fiancé,
on his tractor,
envisioned
a faceless bride
walking towards him.

It was prophetic, she said,
how he saw her face.

Stabbed, my husband implodes.
He will not
tolerate this marriage
and I, steeped in anguish
and fear, cannot.

Hell Bent: A Working Weekend

We have not met the fiancé. The image: my daughter
as chattel with babies on her hip. We locate an exit
counselor from Philly. David, red-haired, lanky,
unpacks bags full with videotapes, pamphlets,
our-soon-to-be bible: Lifton's *Thought Reform
& The Psychology of Totalism*. Cokes, coffee, sandwiches,
cookies non-stop. We rap our brains in hell-bent grit,
read out loud, cram as if for final exams.

We break to watch *The Wave*, a true story, a high school teacher's
experiment, proclaims absolute rules—*strength through discipline,
community, action*. He dictates: a dress code, a salute to one another
in and out of school with a Nazi-style hand gesture. Those who fail?
Reported, tried. The guilty? Relegated to the library.

In four days, the experiment ferments, catalyzes suspicion.
Students denounce one another, cast shadows of *Sicherheitsdienst*.

The Pretense: Act 1

Morning of the visit, my breakfast cold.
Can we push the wedding date ahead?

I pace until the dusty Ford truck rumbles
into our driveway. Dressed in blue overalls,

the farmer has a soft face, ill at ease
as he greets me. At lunch it seems surreal

to ask about their wedding and for Maya to speak
of bridesmaids, a maid of honor, her wedding

dress designed by the women of the group
as if I were not the mother-of-the-bride.

Her father encourages the farmer
to talk—

a dairy farm, a position in the church, the wedding.
I choke up, interrupt—

I need time to get used to this idea.
Maya's eyes lock onto the farmer's,

a supplicant's plea.
The long silence slows our breaths

until he declares, *A delay is in order.*

Journal Entry: Another Lunch

Long drive to a weathered farm. Greeted by farmer's parents,
elder son, the couple. The mom, a jittery-talker, serves sliced
deli chicken, soft white buns, pickles. The dad takes me aside,
I'd certainly be worried if my daughter went off to college
to marry a dirt-poor farmer. He questions the church—
wife belongs; he does not. Bowled over when he says,
Their no-touch relationship seems odd, even unnatural.

The farmer walks us down the block, shows off
what's to be his and Maya's crumbling house.
I feel Maya's lungs closing off in that barren un-heat.

Thankful—the wedding's on pause until late fall. We're planning
an August intervention but first, must meet Maya's pastor
at the compound and visit her community.

The Pretense: Act 2

At the gate, a guard in grey
asks our names, scans the list.

We're met by a soft-spoken man,
a believer in two worlds.

A pastor of Jews for Jesus,
he speaks of Dorian,

about Christ's charity
while bragging about buildings,

new or renovated—
Dorian's chapel, radio station,

the swimming pool, its concrete,
half poured, earth flung,

funded by a millionairess
now suing.

We meet a couple, both
mental health counselors,

who boast of inviting
folk off the street

to join in prayer with the others.
The woman sits too close,

speaks of the privilege
of being with Jews,

the same blood
as our savior.

As she reaches and strokes
my hands, I do not recoil.

The Pretense: Act 3

Nightfall, a Jews for Jesus service.
Maya, on guitar, leads us in song.
The thought of her leaving, to drive
to a cottage in Maine, holds us.

The farmer blesses
as she enters my car,
sleeping the long miles
of yellow lines to where
my sister, her husband,
my brother wait with David.

She hesitates
as her dad speaks
of his decision
to invite an expert
explain her choices.

She listens, we all listen
to this man as he tells
of his escape from a cult.

When he finishes,
Maya bolts to where David sits,
points her index finger
within a smidge of his nose, says,

You. Who are you?
I want to speak with you. Alone.

Hard

The first four days, Maya's mind
  opens and closes like
    a shutter caught in a swift wind.

At times, she challenges
  hard. At other times,
    goes mute.

The hardest moment—
  when David brings forth
    a major research report

stating Dorian's claim
  of anointment by God,
    in no way true.

Maya flees
  to our room. Her brother
    reads the report,

knocks
  on the door, speaks to her
    as no one else can.

You know the kind of guy he is.
  Growing up, we knew guys like him.
    They talk the talk,

use words to impress,
  lie to get what they want.
    We did it ourselves as kids,

but this is big time, a big lie—
  about your life, not just talk.
    Hearing her brother's voice,

its ring so familiar, Maya rejoins
  to read the report, watch *Jonestown.*
    Jim Jones, leader of the People's Temple,

his voice, ear worming on loudspeakers,
  during meals, work in the fields, sleep,
    We are under attack, pursued.

The Turning

My stoic sister Sara
leaps from her chair—

Look around.
Who are we to you?
We are your family.

As Maya steps into Sara's arms,
her mind switches to the farmer,
how they had fantasized
her family might kidnap her,
(a Romeo and Juliet plot
with the twist that if she were missing,
the farmer would follow).
If she does not return by morning,
the farmer will set out,
begin a search.

David is insistent we watch
Jimmy Swaggert:
how he uses words,
gestures, to disabuse.
Maya again in retreat,
her brother, worried—

Where's the old Maya?
I want some feeling.

You were wonderful during my hard time.
You put me together.

What happens if you leave?

Her answer: *No one leaves.*

Hunter-Farmer on the Move

Maya, wanting to stay, calls the farmer,
says she is safe
but needs more time,
Will call again
a day or two later.

Rage—
at Portland's police station,
his missing-person report
dismissed. He cannot state
the color of his lost maiden's eyes,
her hair, even her height.

Three Former Faith Seekers

share stories of lust,
Dorian's greed, his travel
for pleasure, his fear
of persecution, the lies
that drove them out.

Nighttime, Maya and me,
in the same bed,
a cautionary measure.

Her head on my lap,
nestled in,
deep in sleep,
she bolts up, cries out—
What took you so long?

Herding

One day she will tell her fiancé,
but now, it's time
to leave this place, to go
to somewhere safe.

We worry: is the farmer alone?
Does he have members with him?

We take a round-about route,
switch our car for my brother's
and on to Portland's Jetport.

We move together like a herd.
At the ticket counter, four across,
to *Unbound,* for re-entry, Iowa City.

A bookstall beckons.
Maya slides a finger along
a row of book spines.
It feels strange to choose.

After Unbound

On the screened porch
sheltered by rhododendrons
past their bloom,
their words private,
Maya engages with the farmer
to warn him again
of the Faith Seekers
and to say good-bye.

In the end, he rages off—
red-faced, silent
refusing to take back the ring.
I worry she'll lift the ring to light,
slip it on,

but Maya wraps
the cross-shaped diamond
into a wide strip cut
from the skirt she wore
as Maria in *West Side Story*,
when as a girl of seventeen,
she performed
in her soprano voice,
One Hand, One Heart.

Epilogue

Let us mourn
the children
wrested away
as well
their families
who each day
lament
their living deaths.

About the author

Photo by Marvin Snider

Faye Snider, MSW, MFA, a retired clinical social worker and family therapist, writes true stories in narrative and verse forms. She has published professional pieces titled *Holocaust Trauma and Imagery: The Systemic Transference into the Second Generation, Poetry: A Way to Bear Witness*, and *Rescue from a Cult: A Living Death in the Family*. She earned an MFA in creative writing from the Solstice Creative Writing Program and has published personal narratives in *Alimentum, Sugarmule* and *Boxy*. Her poem, *Cousin Lewie*, received first prize in The Chautauqua Writing Center Poetry Contest in 2021. Find more of her poetry in *Ibbetson Press, 200 New Mexico Poems*, and *Lily Poetry Review*.

9 781957 755274